When You Were Just a Heartbeat

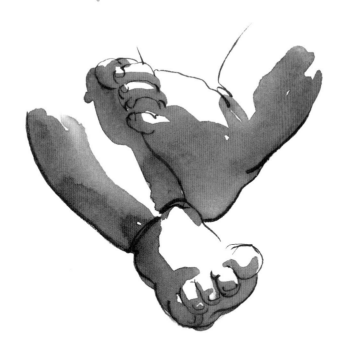

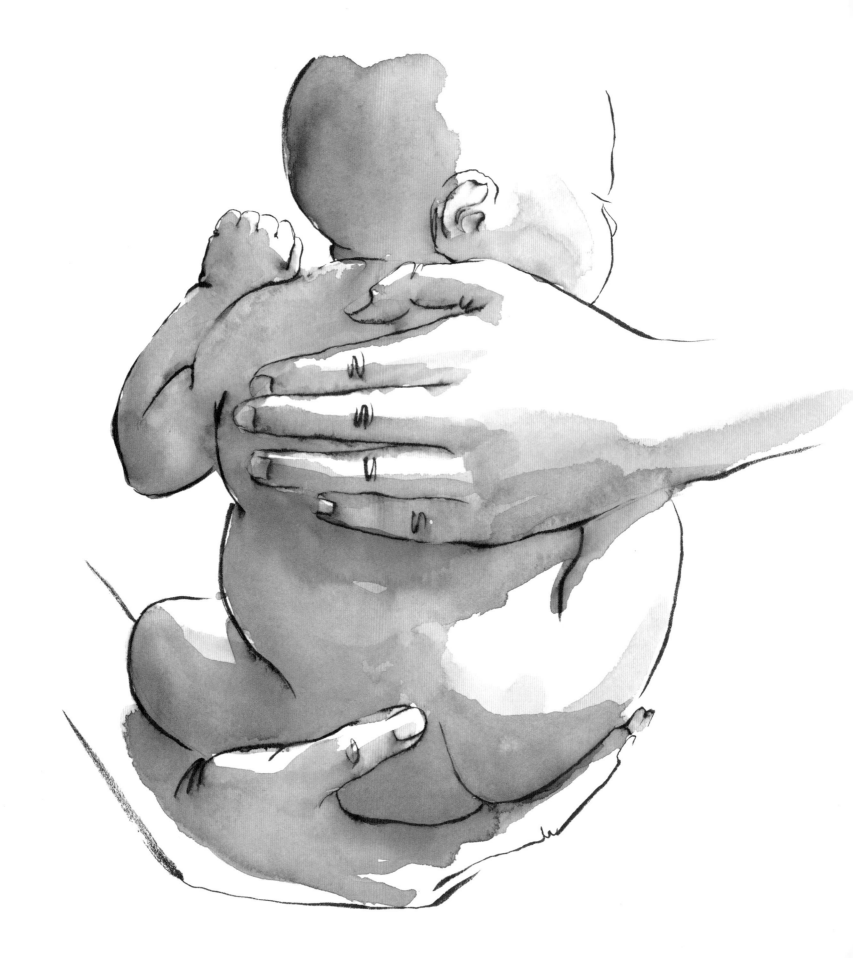

When You Were Just a Heartbeat

Laurel Molk

LITTLE, BROWN AND COMPANY

New York ❧ An AOL Time Warner Company

First Edition

Library of Congress Cataloging-in-Publication Data

Molk, Laurel.
　　When you were just a heartbeat / Laurel Molk—1st ed.
　　　　p. cm.
　　Summary: Loving parents describe for their baby what it was like awaiting
the time of birth.
　　ISBN 0-316-57980-7
　　　[1. Babies—Fiction.　2. Parent and child—Fiction.]　I. Title.

PZ7.M7334 Wh 2002
[E]—dc21　　　　　　　　　　　　　　　　　　　　2001029353

10 9 8 7 6 5 4 3 2 1

Book design by Alyssa Morris

SC

Manufactured in China

The illustrations in this book were done in watercolor on Arches hot press.
The text was set in Lilith and the display type was hand-lettered by John Stevens.

To Richard, Wendy, David, Peter, and Becky for showing me
that babies are amazingly fun.

And to Jack Andrew, who defines amazing and fun.

And thank you to Ilana and Lori for such courageous crits; to Alyssa,
Ginger, and Maria—an incredible combination of talent; to Amy, Dana,
Debbie, and Jane—the best librarians ever; and to Peter for all the
Cadbury awards and so much more.

When you were just a heartbeat
we fell in love with you. The days were
short, the nights were long, and
the snow fell softly.

As you grew, winter turned to spring. The pond melted, and the ducks returned from far, far away.

While you were growing fingers and toes, the salamanders, wood frogs, and spring peepers all migrated under the cover of darkness as the rain poured down from the heavens above.

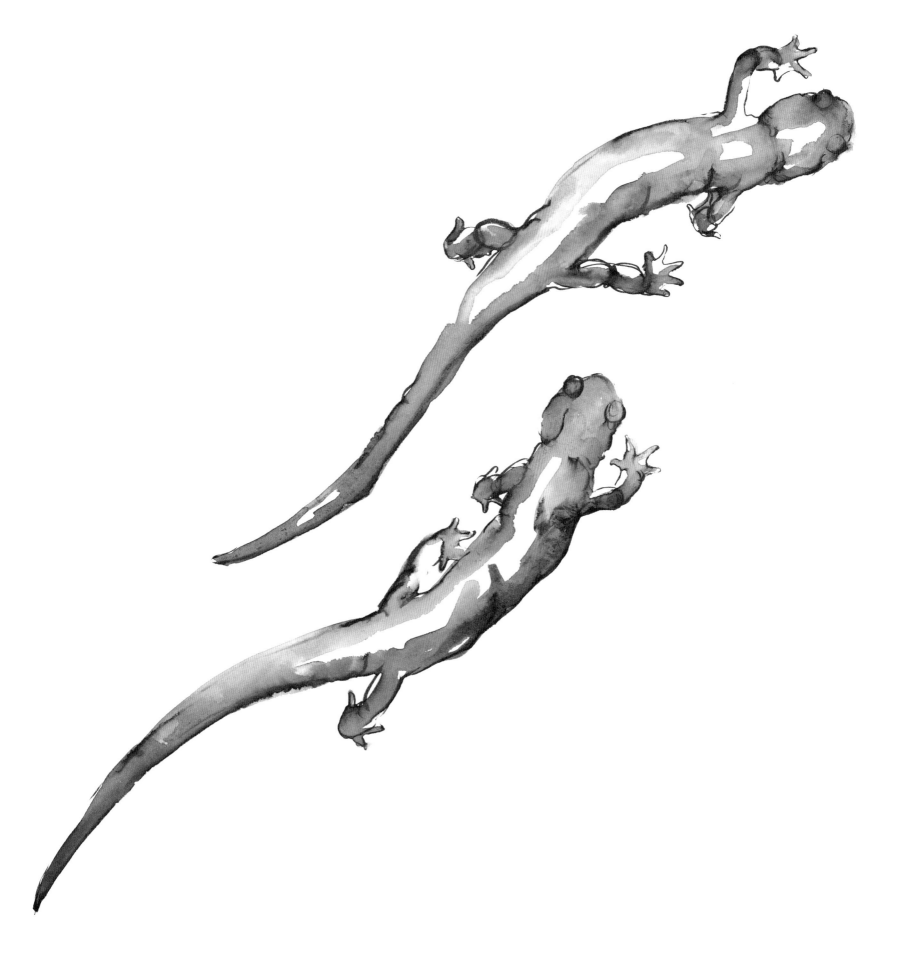

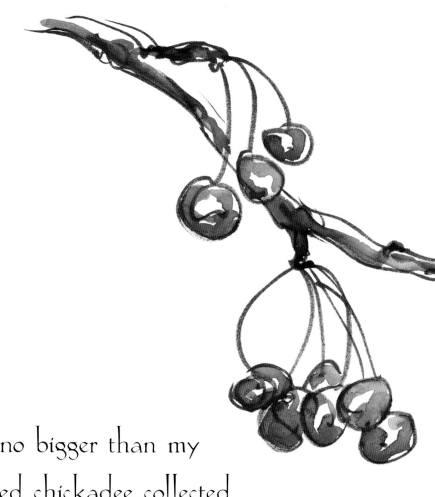

When you were no bigger than my palm, the black-capped chickadee collected twigs and tufts of grass and even bits of string to build its nest.

As you were punching and kicking within, new lambs were being born on the farm and taking their first wobbly steps toward their mamas.

At last you could hear us. It seemed
as if the birds were celebrating—calling
back and forth and spreading
their wings for flight.

Around the time you opened your eyes for the first time, the irises were standing straight and tall—a purple parade.

While you were busy doing forward rolls, the squirrels were scampering about, gathering the first acorns to stash away for the long winter ahead.

When you were too big to roll
over, the pumpkins were fat
and round on the vine.

And when you were born we all rejoiced. And we'll always keep on loving you.